at the shops

A FIRST PICTURE DICTIONARY

Words by Alison Wright
Pictures by Gerald Hawksley

At the shops

shoe shop

clothes shop

supermarket

pet shop

toy shop

bakery

sports shop

The supermarket

- basket
- handle
- safety harness
- child seat
- trolley
- wheel
- carrier bag

orange
apple
lettuce
tomato
potato
banana
pear
cucumber
carrot

sign
shopping list
bags
scales

The supermarket

- cereal
- bread
- biscuits
- butter
- cola
- crisps
- baked beans
- pasta
- jam
- orange squash
- cat food
- dog food
- sugar
- flour

eggs	rice	yoghurt	milk
fish fingers	chicken		cheese
ice cream	peas	sausages	flowers
pizza	coffee	sweets	

The supermarket

toothpaste

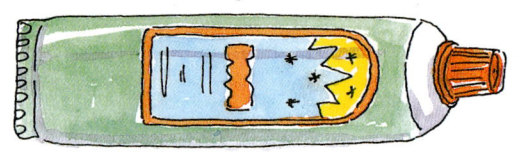

toilet rolls

tissues

bubble bath

shampoo

soap

kitchen rolls

light bulbs

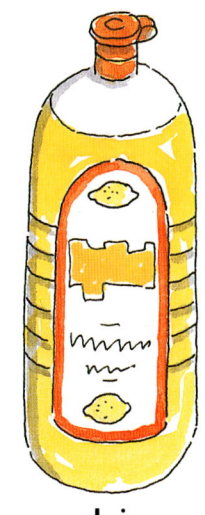

washing-up liquid

dishcloths

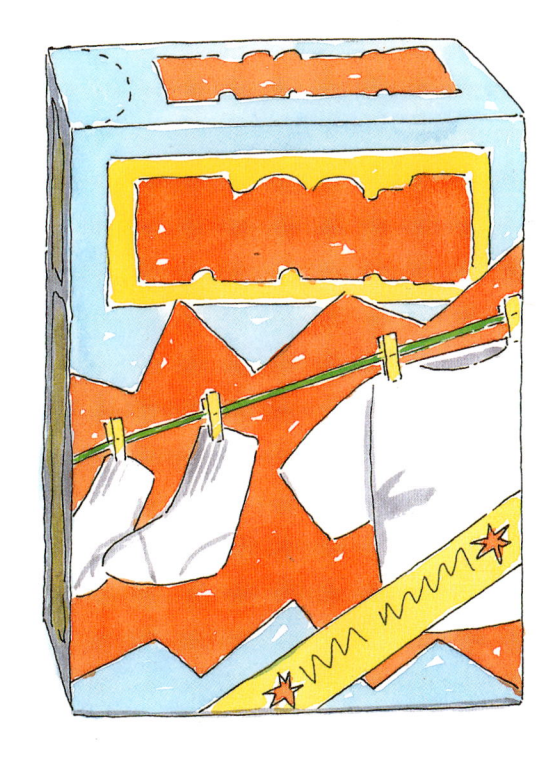

washing powder

dusters

polish

At the checkout

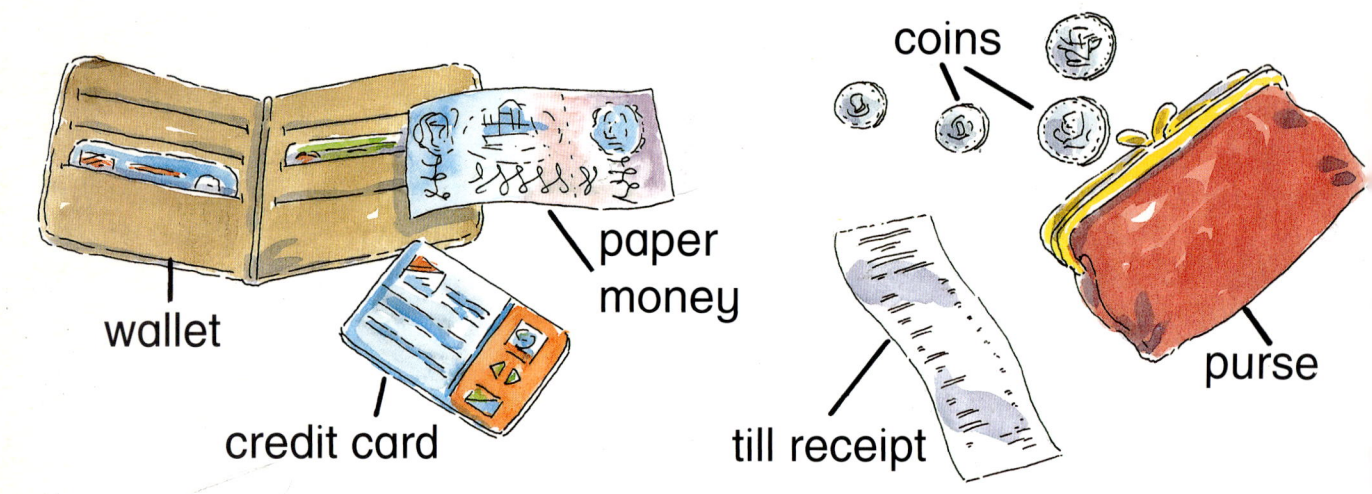

- wallet
- paper money
- credit card
- coins
- till receipt
- purse
- conveyor belt
- bar code reader
- till
- checkout assistant

At the car park

exit

barrier

parking bay

ticket machine

trolley park

Clothes shop

vest

sweatshirt

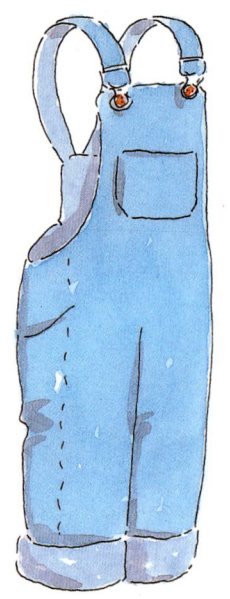

dungarees

knickers

leggings

shirt

T-shirt

jumper

party dress

denim jacket

jeans

coat

changing cubicle

coat hanger

security tag

mirror

dress rail

Shoe shop

boots

lace

sandals — buckle — leather

shoes

velcro

trainers

sole — heel

canvas — rubber

socks

shoe box — foot gauge — polish

Sports shop

- tennis racket
- tennis ball
- football
- golf club
- golf ball
- football strip
- track suit
- table tennis bat
- football boots
- cricket bat
- baseball bat
- swimming trunks
- holdall

Pet shop

- hamster
- gerbil
- exercise wheel
- mouse
- bird table
- bird feeder
- aquarium
- drinking bowl
- straw
- hay
- sawdust
- birdcage
- hutch
- drinking bottle

tropical fish

budgerigar — perch

guinea pig

goldfish

rabbit

parrot

rabbit food

dog leads

dog collars

chocolate treats

clockwork mouse

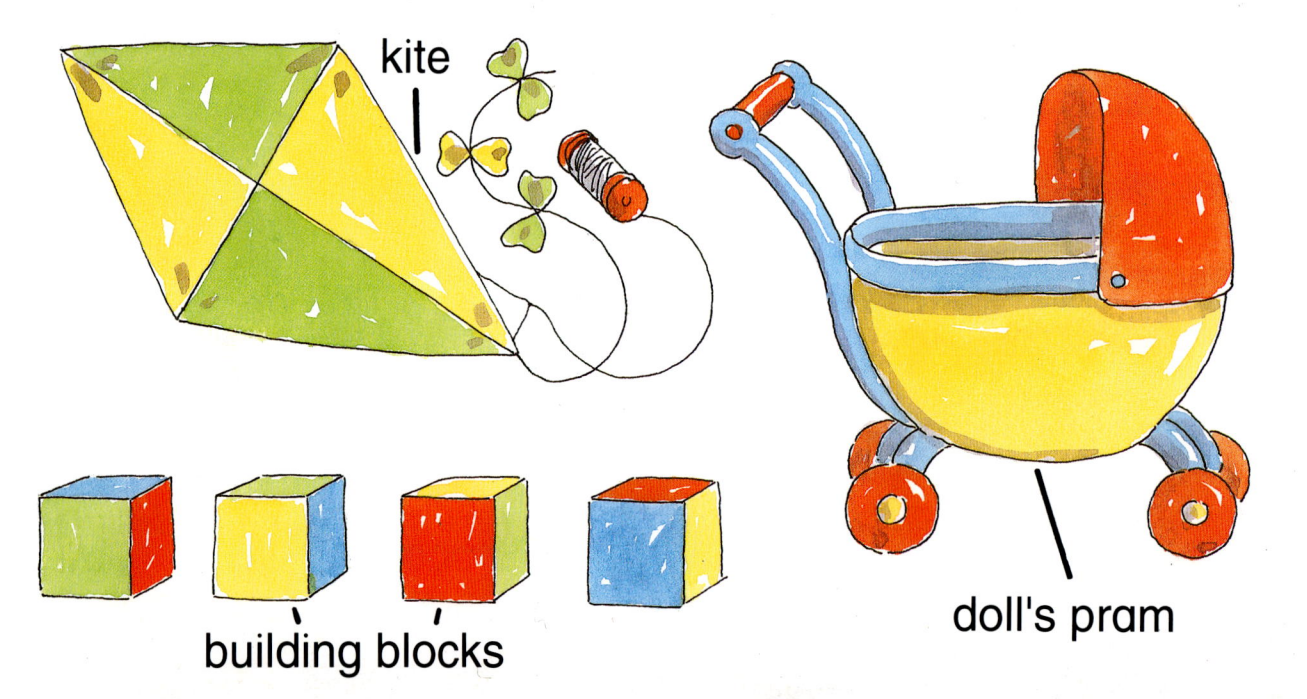

Toy shop

- teddy
- robot
- doll
- doll's house
- kite
- doll's pram
- building blocks

- book
- skipping rope
- ball
- boat
- aeroplane
- car
- train

The bakery

- cherry
- cream
- cake
- gingerbread man
- eclair
- currant bun
- jam tart
- swiss roll
- cupcake
- danish pastry